NO CHERRY TIME

Jennie Feldman
NO CHERRY TIME

PUBLICATIONS
2022

Published by Arc Publications,
Nanholme Mill, Shaw Wood Road
Todmorden OL14 6DA, UK
www.arcpublications.co.uk

978 1910345 81 8 (pbk)

Design by Tony Ward
Printed in Great Britain by TJ Books,
Padstow, Cornwall

Cover illustration:
Detail from 'Pardes Hanna-Karkur'
(oil on canvas)
© Ardyn Halter 1995

ACKNOWLEDGEMENTS
Poems in this collection have appeared in *Oxford Poetry*,
Poetry Review,*PN Review*, *Stand*, *Times Literary Supplement*.

Arc Publications UK and Ireland Series:
Series Editor: Tony Ward

for my friends

CONTENTS

I

II

I

BRIGHT SIDE (DETAIL)

What sweet rot you talk, honeysuckle
flagging on a wall
to fruit, done blooming.

Memories one by one being
lost and still
your pungent homilies in passing.

WATCHTOWER

God no
but a likeness or two

up there watching you
watch ribbed strays amble and pee

on old trees giving up
no man's olives

as cloud shadow
slips across quick as Elijah

on the run south
(fearful stopover

in these hills Jezebel
breathing hard in a nightmare)

bright ghosts with baskets
– no Wall no razor wire –

stooping to pick
khubeizeh's rounded leaves

khubeizeh 'mallow' (Arabic)

12

NEWS

Something's shrunk the pond by half,
too few pickings in the silted muck.

How do they paddle this shallow life,
the sheeny drake and his tidy duck?

Something's lost now friends have flown,
slick weeds, sly roots gaining ground

where reflections used to match their own
deeply. Strangers in a strange pond

– motes in the hunter's narrowed eye
the day they rise and row across the sky.

HOW TO TRANSLATE

… dull curses from the carpet seller
deadweight days rolled on one shoulder
and you not buying; life's foul luck
the muck of it, the ruck he's stuck in

… trucked-in olive trees when you ask
habibi, are you lonely, do you mind
playing traffic island, standing in
for belonging?

… mynah birds flown
free, mimicking
blackbirds they're evicting,
getting it (anyone listening?)
brazenly wrong

… what it's meant to say
forty feet up   the tree on a column
gaunt limbs
praying for heaven
knows what
(dangling water-pipes
flinch in the wind, dry olives
pelt the ground)

… the gaping sparrow full grown
on a ledge, hopping back
and forth, no song

… yellow-pink haze, chemico-
apocalyptic – what you
call sunset and ride into

ROOM 67

*Edward Lear's painting 'Jerusalem', the Ashmolean
Museum, Oxford*

Dogged pilgrim hooked
on the transcendents, up you trudge
for the staggered sweep – bedrock
declivities, shade gashing the wadi –

to that walled trick of light on the ridge.
Climb the path, nothing to stop you,
from the bottom right-hand corner
believe in olive trees with no future.

Fine lines – craquelure or goat tracks –
nearby grazers must have followed;
a place now riddled with roads
concrete, contrarieties undreamt

where two robed goatherds – their easy
belonging given, archaic – have
no time for you. How their sitting rhymes
with the slope, blood-red blobs for poppies.

RIFLEMAN'S NIGHT

The moon takes delight
in all, death and life

mist spreading over
like a white river

the hillsides crawling
and not with goblins

but pissed-off riflemen:
shit, they mumble,

can't see what's where
– d'you believe in war?

Henri Thomas

HEY, SHADOW

Hey, Shadow – will you let go now?
Cherry stain season, all the songs thickbooted,
falling in. Here come night cats –

death on wheels by a whisker missed
has dumped more names in the dark,
barely lived in, difficult to pronounce.

IN PASSING

dinned by news you all but miss
lime trees wholly dizzy with bees
pale flowers seized, rifled, released
in innocence as you walk by

LA MANIÈRE NOIRE

I

So tight the spiral staircase, head
loses sight of feet till you cork-pop
into a gauzy room, walls billowing
floor nothing to be sure of
even as half the ceiling peels
clean off, its flayed thickness hanging,
unfinished business.

II

Whose sleeping child is this
we carry by turns and where
are we trudging? Stark hills
familiar, etched over how many years
out of black by sharp
staccato ricochets scraping the night.
Fireworks, target practice.

III

Woke myself croaking
a shout, foolish.
Gone the small crowd
I'd stood with, the bulldozer coming.
Listen. Already next door
a mason's chisel chipping the silence
down to its heart of stone.

FACES

From a bench he stares at cars on Beitar Street.
The Lord's word thumps great coughing out of his beard
but Jeremiah says nothing, ancient mud on his feet
wrists chafed from the rope. Even if he's heard
the news, seen the outsize flags turning day to night,
he'll raise no alarm – off-duty, intent on
a vision of grace: rapt
faces, new drivers rounding the bend
in both languages. Anything possible. Here
they practise, where city sheers off to desert.

NOCTURNE

Under cover of darkness, stealth
not your thing, lumbering out there snouting
through needle-drift, this your neolithic domain

for night rites nothing to do with us, as if
your hunger's truer than ours and the pines'
knuckled grip you've bared and slobbered over

hadn't begun with the planter – gone to earth
too early – patting in saplings your height
half a lifetime ago. So much to dig up

on this steep patch of hill the roots and rocks
– gaudy with fallen pomegranates – hold back.
No matter. One blink of your ancient eye

gives the scale. And are you still there? Hard to say
now the wind's risen and tangled branches
rasp and croon with the weight of the undropped dead.

NO CHERRY TIME

Otherwise lovely the branches
  flung in rows you walk – see
   early spurts of blossom, how bright
    on the flinty soil, this hillside
     studded with O's of ochre stumps
      giving up (count the rings)
their half-score years. How the light
  hums with the busy chainsaw
   down where the orchard ends, where
    last winter's knee-deep snow
     floored you under a budding sky.
And you saw it, the greatest show
  on earth, umpteen mid-pirouette sylphides
   blurring this slope, ecstatic stillness
    for applause. And now
     they've dropped – limbs
      awry – how to forget the dance?
Among stray twigs one stumbling bee
  looks lost – wasn't this the spot? –
   fumbles, staggers, takes off
    with the bad news to ghost hives
     under the cypresses.
                              Pick up
remnants of old seasons, black
  as biblical olives (the stalks insisting
   cherry, cherry!) in your palm, making much
    of the wrist's brief throbbing,
     the contrapuntal whistle and flit

of migrant warblers in and out
of the green's dismembered rustling.

This thin air we stand on where
the pit's already plotted, the deadpan
concrete.
(Out of a fold
in the hill a hatted man strides, gives
no answer to your greeting.
One of you doesn't exist.)
Stone
on stone on stone; the hands
that laid this terrace wall
long gone to bone, half-wild almonds
rooting its base so the world
won't slide. To be
in no time clawed out, knocked flat.

Heavy the leaving, crammed pockets
clicking with almonds as you walk,
a good stone in your hand to crack them.
Chew on what we're losing
as night comes. Find
true north – pinned in a blink
unsinking.
How long
till the bulbul pipes up, tunes
a dawn chortle to perfection, makes nothing
of faint rumbles, scrapings, peeping reversals
where a hillside's being shaken
out of the dream?

23

DRY SEASON

leaves' tomfoolery at daybreak
  – rain? leap up rush out
     barefoot
       for nothing
again from heaven

         O high wild geese –
    and the speck
        of you left standing

where a blackbird thwacks a snail
gulps its small adventure
         sweep away parched olives
plant more bulbs

We are past the age of complaining;
Besides, what would we complain about?
Long since weaned from the mother whale.
We have been in the throat of the war whale
And it spat us back onto the shore.
Peevish or proud, we are past the age.

I, says Jonah, end sentences with a full-stop.
And the capital at the start of each line is only because
It looks better that way, any printer will tell you.
It's different, of course, for someone being read to
Who doesn't mind about capitals either way.
And yet, Lord – though this certainly isn't
To raise my voice against the Almighty.
Rather against myself, chewing on my folly
Bitter-tasting in my near-toothless mouth.
Against my madness and this empty self
That makes of me
A whale of vanity, balloon of wind.

But in the Lord's absence I sit and grow sad.

What, though, what would Jonah complain of?
I'm alive, says Jonah, not very alive
Since the Holy Spirit visits so rarely and briefly
I am alive my mouth still full
Of the sea and the beast's pungent fluids
And not yet recovered from sea-sickness
But in sum there's no saying it's all going well
And if it's not, just keep going.

Palms, in the green sky of birds of passage
At the water's edge, evening still blazing
Washed up on the coast of Brazil I lifted my eyes
and thank the Almighty who holds me cupped in his hand.

It's not so much that I blame myself
And I'm not trying to plead my case either.
What! I haven't much lied, have never killed and
Almost never had such thoughts; otherwise, for sure
An idler, a wheedler, at times a whiner
In short not someone of great or particular interest.
O metaphysical liquefaction, buddhistic drowning
O dispensation from making an unneeded person
O weariness and secret longing to be lost for good
In the innermost dark of some definitive whale.
Watchman, tell us the night's end.

Good deal, good quality, good fortunes
Good use of my rights,
Good standing, good all-rounder, good boy,
Good life, good for nothing,
When things go wrong, just keep going.
Ah interesting times, make a note
ah, the self has its interest
but what of someone who has settled down, who lives in-between
who hasn't enough love of Self or God
who's been spat from the dark of his private whale
on an empty shore where talking to God is beyond him
what, in his case, can he do?

Jean-Paul de Dadelsen

SITE

Pandaemonium rising
behind you – hard-hatted
angels flaming torch

and no going
back to the wild fig days
of trespass and caperbush

leaping madly
in summer's loose walls.
Nothing of that

in the masterplan
and no appeal.
Pines gone, small cries

swifts coming back
unfailing as love
from their far winter.

MAPPA MUNDI

Where the point jabbed and held,
swinging a battlemented wall
round the self-centred city

3D scans reveal the hole
(belly-button of the world
said the prophet, bull's eye

for His fury) and calf skin
gently hummocked as in a dream
of pastures beside still waters.

LEAVING

Sky of a sudden threaded with their rasping –
urgent, fading. Did they start it, the wild geese?

Next door the sax player changes his tunes.
'Tequila', 'Autumn Leaves' give way to zealous
hits. One day, silence. Nothing since, not even
scales.

"Days grew hotter and drier, urban
centres collapsed, people moved out to the
countryside…" Pocket-size storm god with
raised arm. Take note.

Every thought boat-shaped – already the
planks, the sailcloth in place – *forever scanning /
the stars, the Pleiades and the Ploughman.* Nightly
from the flat above, rough seas churning.

Upstairs the tap's turned off. Faint squeak
against enamel, a too-shallow bath. Thud is the
hauling out. Briefly jangled bedsprings.

First light means testing the rigging, checking
the rudder. In the stairwell greetings exchanged
with neighbours who never know it's the very
last time.

II

Being knee-deep in river dazed
with here and now I and the cattle
– we've ambled then full-on hoofed it
to facing banks – stand mirrored.
Minnows flick tiny transmissions
poplars tremble. Gusts, horripilations
of a calm that is and isn't. Squawks
trills, fluted cadenzas pin me here un-
utterably. River, as you were saying –

TO OXFORD STATION

Just past All Souls we veer
to high mountains
an accented village pinned by words
on the brink. Fierce longing
creases his grey stubble:
Even in summer
water like ice from the tap
wild figs plums strawberries
mountain tea
good for everything, yes, but who
doesn't grow old? Next spring
he will go back. Or the next.
This city already a dot
on a speckled island, exile's profile
beside me circling
the Sea Between the Lands –
Here we are, he says mildly.
Turns off the meter.

ROCK EDGE RESERVE

whose land have I lit on now?
THE ODYSSEY

Call it a day dear gods & float me
off this reef. It's not in the story not even
at sea – these quarried ridges
corals shells gastropods drily

snag each sailing thought
ankle-deep in daisies. Poppies
buttercups. Saying them
out loud to catch the drift but nothing

doing. Must you dear gods always
clamp the blue & vanished
music to my ear? Mighty chunks
moonstruck in nettles & ferns

stuck into walls like tombstones. What if
tonight I pour a libation hoist
a sail? O then the scribbled wake
as the roads of the world grow dark.

OTHERWISE

To think of it framed high
in beeches. Is to see
not the deer but the river

of us racing below
undrinkable as it watched.
The deer the lovelier. How

its thirst transfigured
briefly the M40, how
we flowed.

LEAR'S BIRDS

from a series of imaginary birds painted by Edward Lear

The Pink Bird

How to get a grip – scant-toed
chick number twenty-one
at Bowman's Lodge (Holloway)
dislodged unfledged pink
& clueless – sixty-odd years on?

Eye skyward, whence come
fantastical figments
marvellous skews that fly
thin air against our limits.
Flap-flap *absolomly alone*

but chirping – to every passing
aloneness – larky fables
to take us in. Look: *There is*
no more trouble ahead
Sorrow or any such thing.

The Black and White Bird

Lifted birdily out of the sober
quirks of sadness, not to be weighed down.
Forget the palette, the easel-hours stuck
sitting *like a petrified gorilla* –

here's quick strokes, dark washes.
Poised ambiguities: landing /
taking off? One bright eye unfailing
dares an old man's

wingsprung bespectacled
spherical & bearded
comic-poetical self to find
grace in the fine uncertainties.

THE CRIMSON BIRD

One rolled eye for heaven's sake
this branch-pose nothing
but jiggery-clownery

too disabused (by c. 1880)
to parrot the likes of Parrots
– feather-perfect, Latin –

yet kindly, keeping
the ironies tight-
beaked, tucked in brightness.

THE GREY BIRD

No bright rhyme for this backward glare,
the oboe-squawk half throttled
with hindsight's effort.
Barely, acrobatically, hanging on.
Is it in the way fear squiggles
a frown and overdoes the eye's
black brow that we glimpse relief?
Gravity resisted against the odds
the Morbids, poor sight, perennial
Demon seizures (x's in diaries).
Grey tones, pigeon-haunted
– *no bird more beautiful* – rinsed
to a bluesy defencelessness. But

(Oh! W! X! Y! Z!
Did it never come into your head
That our lives must be lived elsewhere)

even a lifetime's habit of flight
– inward & out & south & east –
the rollicking tales and painted lands
will not fully translate the cry: *I am*
mortissimo in body & soul…

                              Yet
seeing out the moment: headspun words
& feathered lines; no more fervent flying.

EXTRA

I

Listen, you are and you aren't.
Yes, to make the action believable
moment by moment; otherwise, no.
Today: expectation – part joy
part disbelief. Don't overdo it. The feeling
barely surfaces, but we see it.
Don't blink. There should be
infinity in your gaze.

II

The weather, Plato, whatever
it takes to look like friends
having coffee. And no big gestures –
you hardly figure till the sobbing
makes you turn, brings you in.
Then puzzled, embarrassed; but
pain too, recognition. Indirectly you
heighten the drama.

III

So you're leaning to look
back a last time. Not sad or happy,
more uncertain. That's it – ongoing
uncertainty. Compose your face
with dark and light, to reflect the story.
The final shot is what stays. Like those
Russian horses in the rain by the river.
If words help, keep them to yourself.

ONCE UPON A TIME...

Without ambiguity you cannot go deep enough
NURI BILGE CEYLAN, DIRECTOR

Who's guilty? Who knows. Traipsing the hills
with questions. *Cut! – You're not looking* at
anything, you are looking within. Okay.

This could go on. Days, a lifetime. Trees
complicit in moonlight, not telling. Now just
Anatolian trees. And a man sobbing. Such

is the pain when lamplight and tinkling
tea glasses enter and she, lit angel, stoops
to each in the weary dark with her tray.

Not a word – maybe a mumbled thanks –
wind like a wind-machine turned up, barking
faint in the valley as I step outside, head home.

OPEN NOTES

as if this green
the puzzle of it
sway and layer
rain needling the river
could catch our drift

*

coots don't care
leaf rot inching
a cold idea of summer
one way or the other

*

O great oaks revolving rootedness
keep us in sight till mist
and curve rub us out

*

cockerel's cramped arpeggio shut up
in the hen house
morning no glory

*

we on the bluff parenthetical
in bracken

boats rocking
just enough to prove the haven

    *

lighthouse
what distances you keep
for dark

backdrag yes but
a tidal inching

oho bladderwrack
undead groping

slumped blue
boat cocky again

salve! rising
crabwise sea

rock bottom
forgotten

Midnight foxy wheeze more sob
than bark startles you. The red-eyed man
propping a bewilderment
against the pub's seaward wall till dawn,
black shrimps crated for Spain
hopping, clicking their agonies.

Danger Unprotected cliffs Rogue waves
Springy on heather, hat sprigged
(bog myrtle against the midges) you spy
beyond the plump blackberries
a figure – no, a standing stone
marker for the faceless drowned.

Staggered constellations
let up dawn on a stippled grey –
peninsula fudged to island, you're hardly
here. Not to startle the long-billed
turnstones flipping pebbles, be still.
Imagine purpled hands rinsed by the sea.

ZEUS

Gloom-eyed god bullish in a meadow
we saw you, how you swaggered over,
she browsing, new calf tugging below,
to sniff super-searchingly at her rear
and slowly, upper lip pulled high,
tilt your know-all grin to the sky.
Jokes like that the gods will never share.

MUSIC NIGHT

Where it ends, lopped off
– island-isle-i – the sea
westward takes over, pulls
down a late sun, Otherworld-wise

this stone circle a thinking place
and *Dies irae* thundering on
unerasable from the airport bus:
Dublin City Ghost Tours

'the real thing'. But the bay
levels with you its waters.
Herons, high tide… rabbit –
aren't we in this together

thin soil riddled with tangent
bolt-holes, fiercer gorse
where the cliff leans out
forgetting? And sky

takes our small measure,
scumbles and hangs into depths
its pearl and slate, edging
brilliant. Always this

to squint at, stumbling out
of the dark, the day's song found,
quill pens scratching it down
where the thick-walled Bardic School

keeps its ruined lookout. And where
– not to dither, night falling – from here?
Blackness as sea, or a scrambled
shortcut to music at the Tin Whistle.

TRESPASS

Unblinking swallow on a wire in a shed
knockout silence between us, how on earth

are we? Your natty compilation of sky
and swerve, so precisely tacit, lets it

go without saying. So what if shadows
have blotted the hills, the lookout pines

reeling. Roofed here eye to eye we knot
all those Cretan swoopings, dizzy unburdened

glimpses of harbours, cliffs, and summer trees –
What are you? glares the tapered glyph. Go away.

ON NIGHT ROADS

Ghosted by voices
drum guitar fiddle – lit places
on night roads take you in

and don't. Part of you waits
in the rain not singing
the unfelt words you're belting

out with the shining faces;
would go, but for that canny beat
tapping unguarded spaces.

CONSIDER

Consider the brown rat
coasting the hedges
innocent of loathing

the bibbed white patch
when it perks on its haunches
delicate as a loved thing.

III

CRETE

That a child's clay ox, goggle-eyed
pull-along from the afterlife, trails
some lost joy behind you

and an anchor tall as two men,
puny against the crazed and pocked
seaward Byzantine wall, even so props it,

that they've nailed in a row cast-off doors
in the Evraiki quarter – such things
add up as you lean to pull in the shutters.

EPIC

Παράξενα απόψε με κοιτάζεις [...]
(from a popular Greek song)

You're looking at me strangely tonight... Slumped under fairy lights, Orestes doesn't care. Pours more wine, adds Cola for a steady head, these being terrible times.
BATTLEPROOF says his leather jacket front and back

Dark – a catch, near-sob in her voice – *dark suspicion eats at my insides*
He looks up. The shock-red dress.
It must have been her tapping the quayside, a flame parting the crowd or goddess feigning blindness

Let me die for you... Hand to breast and reaching out –
                    To him? He sits up. Scans the locked night of her eyes
Before my golden dreams are knocked down...

On the curved brushstroke of the shore two helmeted figures – crimson, black – riding as one. White tints for the slim, clasping arms.

UNSPOKEN

Against your palm
        a shuttered wall
the slow dusk
dunks in shadow
        presses back warm.

RITE

for D.

Where the sea thumps and gargles and I'm lost
in thought seeing his chiselled face, its youth
absent under white lights, autumn winter
spring and anemones under the pines
the day he stepped out, every inch benign
coltish in the newness of his walking –

a shout, Greek baritone, startles. Behold
Christos ageless in hat and boots; radiant
he waves, leaps rock to rock, slices limpets
clean off (mute protestation). Now he palms
terrible nakedness, with his penknife
scoops the flesh, mimes quaffing it. *Is for you.*

Five empty shells, two lemons from his trees,
how lightly they assemble the moment.
The giver – that's him, walking the far haze
like water – matches the archaic sign
for 'man'. To think how he laughed, slapped his
    thigh
as I chewed, gulped the transfiguring sea.

Why the long face, Philoctetes?
You and your foot-rot better off here –
figs not men dropping to earth
                              Troy just visible.
But of course you'll sail in the end,
kill and in time be killed.

                         Old story. War
across the water, ships rocking
the dead back to shore.

Island of poppies! they marvelled,
the rookies landing here that spring,
next stop Gallipoli. Then too the Aegean
bolt upright at the ends of alleys
pigeon wings clapping in a mulberry tree
their acrobatic amours.

SAMOTHRACE

words fuddled
by spray over the gunwales
                  cries of landfall

Great Gods
(a straggler pilgrim scribbles)
        will you find time & mercy?

                *

evening's pitch in a gully
                  waterfall spooling
            deep viridian
woken first light by rock-
struck hoofs, dainty slurps

                *

tripping on chiselled slabs
in the hall of the choral dancers
        find an olive's upstart shade
to think in
                  cicadas
sawing the stillness   surf
& gusts through mountain oaks
            wide-winged Nike
breasting the old adversities
                        unburied

            come night
it's the theatral circle, godly
utterances to stand for then
                  stumbling moonless

down the sacred way, dry run
for the unbodied soul   till
        sudden great light dazzles
                epopteia
                exactly here
you'll be okay now
– at sea, in the afterlife –
also, it's said, a better person

                        goat-bleat cicadas

time into stone – go
        reconfigure –
lofty
fluted columns intact
the Great Gods named
    before the undoing
seventeen hundred winters
            to this: masonry stuttering
immortality, the very idea, impossibly
unbroken
                        cicadas

            *

stowed back on deck
the mountain sudden
& sacred behind you
        what's left, what stays
hoped for
like the single dolphin
    to starboard
not everyone saw

folded neat as a lifetime as you step
deeper; what's ahead rolling in
ho-hum nothing of transport.
Who's watching now the eye-level sun
throws shadows in streaks from driftwood,
boats hauled up… *lightness*
of thoughtfulness, l'esprit clair…
How long till it looms, the big one
you'll dive under or else
arms whirring, ride
for the cartwheel hurl of it
flat out as far as the darker shore.

Road then path
then track climbing steeply out
of the world. Not a soul.
Just this likeness scrambling
pausing for breath where tombs capsize
in juniper, oleander.

Riddled names. Chiselled grapes
a finger must trace. Between lions rampant
punched holes let in heaped windsift gold dust.

A gust sweeps down Mount Güllük.
At the signal
blossom breaks formation
hurtles white thousandfold against the tower wall
and drops senseless.
No way, thinks the great commander
squinting up at this eagle's nest.
Packs up, marches off.

Up in the gods rising tier on tier
to our feet. Or is it just me
for relief from the stone seat,
bones still fleshed, articulating
at the joints.
                    What last act
before the quake struck? No telling
from the shaken stage. Lokum
in my pocket for such a moment.
Rosewater to chew against
the vague plain below,
the blur of sea.

Termessos

61

APHRODITE, GARE DE LYON

Had she – stepping down from the ceiling
of Le Train Bleu, past ogling satyrs, cupids,
Sarah Bernhardt forgotten on a wall –

slipped off those shoes (jewelled, vertiginous)
to glide down the banister, rounding its brassy
flourish onto the station platform?

Her furs adore her. Seated still she rises
in blonde wavelets above the brasserie stir
smiling, red wine tipped to sip. She waits

swivels heads from menus, TGV
schedules, dumbshows of drawn-out adieux.
Our little lives. Waiters swerve with sidelong

speculations (those gemmed slopes). And here
he comes, guised against envy, sweating.
Takes her through the stares & murmurs

her bare arm grazing his pink pate
its few combed hairs; pantomime-thick glasses
winking, a give-away spring in his step.

QUAI VOLTAIRE

Carved in stone his scowl could be
up there with the gargoyles on the Pont Neuf.
Crapaud, he growls; reels in a twisting
slip of silver, drops it into a bucket
and waves me off: *Crapaud!* Glints

from tall windows where the great man
took in the scene and died. Heaven lies
in a puddle where two pigeons
drink headfirst, the world blinked out.
Doing it by turns, just in case.

ON THE TGV

The thing is, the angel murmured
– disappearing through that casement,
word given, the moment framed –
to climb out. Find a ticket,
hitch on, skim the land due south
as it swells (on the left) darkly
higher to mountains, vineyards
combing out, farmsteads
in their fields rock-weighted,
the loopy Rhône we leap
again, past silver – blossom? –
on gusted trees, eyesocket caves
in the ridge and the river now
thinning to shoals, braidings
all but over –
        and sudden night
blinds the life of us, deeply
as if no angel, no breath, no
climbing ever out –
        and sky, old blue which art
in heaven, back again, cranes
in their lofty purpose, and that glitter
quite beside ourselves
the sea.

MASSALIA

Wide-bellied wreck
besotted with sea, far-

off Phocaea barnacled
on these timbers

ploughing west low
with wine, olives, a priestess

loaned by Artemis
rounding the headland

unsunk amphorae
lugged ashore and so
it begins.

*

Hermes lodges me four floors up, hangs
divine blues over the Vieux Port, says
no messages, madame. Shadows flat out
like the long dead skim the quayside
file aboard hatted for the round-trip,
Liaisons Maritimes by the hour.

Out and back. Islands, reefs to stern as we
swing sharp east, slower – *3 noeuds max.* –
sage, juniper, myrtle sighing off
the headland, sea slapdash on the rocks,
narrowly through and here's the haven,
XAIRE on a threshold in faded mosaics.

Roof perch from the old days (mine): tight-
beaked gulls slope the air, sprig the boats. Hulls
jigging with light. *Que ma joie demeure*
doodled here in a student notebook
stowed with a bottle of pastis when I sailed
east; the world still wide, blissfully unknown.

Rifleman's Night – p. 16
'Nuit du tirailleur', *Poésies* (Gallimard, 1970)

Canticle of Jonah – p. 25
'Cantique de Jonas', *Jonas* (Gallimard, 1962)

Lear's Birds – p. 37
In the Department of Prints and Drawings at the Victoria and Albert Museum, London. Pen and ink and water-colour, ca. 1880. The birds can be viewed at http://www.nonsenselit.org/Lear/birds/index.html

Massalia – p. 65
The port city of Marseille began as Greek colony around 600 BCE.

JENNIE FELDMAN was born in South Africa, grew up in London and studied French at Oxford. A former award-winning radio producer and presenter, she spent much of her time, until recently, in Jerusalem. She is now based in Oxford.

Her first collection of poems, *The Lost Notebook*, was published by Anvil in 2005, as was *Treading Lightly*, her selection and translation of poems by Jacques Réda. *Into the Deep Street* (Anvil, 2009), an anthology of seven modern French poets which she edited and translated with Stephen Romer, was awarded a Special Commendation by the judges of the 2011 Popescu Prize for Poetry in Translation. Her second collection, *Swift*, also from Anvil, appeared in 2012.